RIYA AARINI

Maral

and the

Wisdom of the Forest:
A Quest for Truth

Maral and the Wisdom of the Forest: A Quest for Truth

Text copyright © 2022 by Riya Aarini

Developmental editing by Rachel Small

Copyediting by Carrie Wicks

This is a work of fiction. Names, characters, businesses, places, events, locales, and incidents are either the products of the author's imagination or used in a fictitious manner. Any resemblance to actual persons, living or dead, or actual events is purely coincidental.

ISBN: 978-1-956496-15-4 (hardcover)

ISBN: 978-1-956496-16-1 (paperback)

ISBN: 978-1-956496-17-8 (eBook)

Library of Congress Control Number: 2022904875

First published in Chicago, Illinois, USA

Visit www.riyapresents.com

Part I: The Journey

Part II: The Return Journey

PART I: THE JOURNEY

1
INSPIRATION FOR THE QUEST

*W*hen the first gleam of golden light cracked the horizon, its glow bathed a small, thatched hut in the middle of a clearing. Bilge, a gnome, set out his basket of handpicked alfalfa, clover, and a bit of dandelion next to the porch, as he always did.

The forest deer came to feed on the fresh greens that morning, as they usually did, and hopped away. But one fawn stayed. Her name was Maral.

The fawn held a meaningful place in Bilge's heart. As a sluggish newborn sick with an infection, Maral was unable to nurse and had a limited chance of survival. So she was abandoned by her mother near the thistles in the woods.

The gnome, who had always called the forest home, stumbled upon the scared, huddling fawn barely peeking her head out of the tall grass. Out of a natural sympathy for the wild and lost, he tended to her illness and cared for her. As the quivering fawn grew in health and strength over the next few months, the gnome was tickled by her emerging playfulness, inquisitiveness, and charm. Their friendship was further strengthened by shared interests. Even at four months old, with white spots dotting her back, Maral asked enough questions to show that she was a deep thinker—like Bilge. And the like-minded always preferred one another.

Maral knelt on the grass outside the hut, tucked her face between her spindly legs, and let her eyelids droop.

Whistling a cheery tune and with a skip in his step, Bilge walked out of his hut and into the fresh air. The gnome's foot-long white beard was one-third of his height and flitted in the breeze. He wore clogs, tiny shoes that fit his equally tiny feet. A copper belt fastened around his stodgy waist held up his red pants, and a pointy moss-colored hat covered his tuft of white hair. He was about to add more greens to the basket when he spotted Maral.

The gnome greeted the fawn with his characteristically chipper tone, "Hello, Maral!" He smiled at her. But when he noticed her glum expression, he stopped in his tracks. "My dear, why do you look so sad?"

Maral's dainty eyes looked up at her trusted friend. "I don't want to be a fawn," she said with a small sob.

"Oh?" said Bilge, moving closer. "What do you want to be?"

Perking up, the fawn said, "A human."

The gnome scratched his chin and cocked his head. "Why is that?"

Without hesitation, Maral replied, "Because, to me, they always seem happy. I've seen the humans who live beyond the edge of the forest. They laugh, smile, and play. I want to feel their lasting happiness."

Bilge replied, "To us, they seem that way. We are shown only a small portion of their complete lives, just as we see only the glow of the moon. There is far more to the full moon than the splendor we see once a month. Anyhow, Maral, you are not one to be sad. I've seen you laugh, smile, and play many times."

Maral, revealing her depth of thought, was quick to answer. "But that kind of happiness suddenly comes and just as quickly goes. There must be more to life than those fleeting moments."

The gnome grunted and pondered the fawn's words before replying. "Oh, I see. Let's go for a walk, Maral."

"Where are we going?" asked Maral, standing up.

"Through our forest, of course, which contains all the plants of the earth. Even the ancient trees, those that have lived thousands of years, have a special place in our forest."

"What are we looking for?"

"We are looking for what we will find," he said.

"But the forest is dark and deep. I would not dare venture into the depths of the forest," said Maral, who, at her tender age, had yet to explore the full expanse of the woods. She looked at the gnome with doubtful, glistening black eyes.

"Maral, are you afraid?" asked the gnome in a slower cadence than usual.

The fawn took a step back, her legs quivering, and vigorously shook her head.

"Now, Maral, it's all right to be afraid," said Bilge patiently.

"Well," she said, "I've heard harrowing stories about vicious creatures at the far reaches of the forest. They're known to snarl, bare a mouthful of sharp fangs, and pounce with terrifying claws."

Bilge paused before answering to explore a gentle yet persuasive reasoning. As he dwelled on a fitting response, he rubbed his chin while his long beard jiggled.

Maral tucked in her head and chuckled at the sight.

"You may choose to come along or not, but know that the search for happiness is an admirable one," said the gnome. "A glistening gem cannot be had without first digging through dangerous mines. The work is long. The work is hard. In the end, holding the desired gem in your hands is worth all the effort. Whether or not you reach your goal, the adventure promised during such a worthwhile quest is the most meaningful and enriching part."

Bilge paused again and looked at Maral with a sideways glance. "Maral, pursuing something of great worth comes with equally great risk."

Maral steadied her trembling legs. "I . . . I'll be brave."

"That's the spirit!" he said, starting to pace. "Now, we will circle through our forest, which contains all life on earth, from east to west and north to south," said the gnome. "We should be back by nightfall."

Maral nodded.

Bilge puttered to his left, then to his right. "Let me grab my lantern," the gnome said. "It's still rather dark at this early hour, and my lantern will also shed light on some natural truths."

He hurried inside his thatched hut, tinkered about for a bit, and returned minutes later carrying his lantern. A canteen holding fresh water was strapped across his shoulder, close to his body.

As the gnome began walking on the unworn grass, Maral hopped alongside him.

"There are a few things you need to know, Maral," said the gnome. In the hazy dawn, the lantern created just enough light to see.

"Our forest contains a wisdom, a knowledge that is delivered to us through the life energies of the trees, the plants, and even the rocks," said Bilge. He lifted his lantern toward Maral to illuminate her face.

The fawn wore a curious expression. "Even rocks?"

"Indeed, my dear. Forest rocks are hardly stone alone."

Walking over scattered pebbles, gnarly tree roots, and tall grasses, the pair created their own path through the clearing. Within minutes, they had ventured into the realm of the trees.

"By the end of our journey, you will see, Maral," said Bilge.

"See what?" she asked.

"How the forest teaches us to be."

2
BE LIKE THE REDWOOD

*B*ilge and Maral trampled along in the stillness of the early morning. The gentle crushing of soft blades of grass under their feet and hooves was the only sound. At this hour, even the grasshoppers remained asleep. The dawn's fresh dew, caught in the light of the gnome's lantern, shimmered like gemstones on the grass and leaves.

The companions had walked barely a hundred feet when they reached the forest's first natural wonder. They stopped and looked up. Holding his lantern close to the bark of the masterpiece of nature, the gnome said, "We're standing in the shadows of a giant. Do you know what it's called?"

Maral had lived in the forest her entire four months of life. She paid attention and loved to learn whenever

Bilge gathered the leaves from nearby plants for his teas or medicinal purposes. So she was certain she knew the names of all the plants around her. Wide-eyed, she responded, "The redwood towers before us!"

Bilge smiled. "Yes, indeed. We are just wee folks under it, yet it is gracious enough to reveal to us boundless truths."

"Like what?" asked Maral.

"If you pay attention, you will come to know." Still holding his lantern against the bark, the gnome said, "Be like the redwood: strong and enduring." He turned to her. "But these columns of ultimate strength don't grow out of the ground this way. Do you know how they start, Maral?"

The fawn shook her head. "No, how?"

"As seeds that are as tiny as the freckles on your nose," said the gnome with a chuckle.

Maral wiggled her nose, as if about to sneeze. "Ah . . . ah!" She took two steps back. "*Achoo!*" She sniffled. "And yet they grow so mighty!"

Bilge laughed. "Gesundheit! Yes, the redwood's growth is a patient one, yet words alone cannot describe the magnificence of these trees of immense fortitude. We stand in the midst of humble titans."

Maral stretched her neck and aimed her gaze at the massive treetops high above. "How long do they live?"

"Only a living thing gifted with strength and patience can thrive for two thousand years, Maral. The redwoods are the noble survivors of the centuries. In the wind and rain and drought—all things our forest bears—the redwood has the strength to thrive. Even once the tree dies, its journey isn't over. The tree returns to the ground and nourishes the soil, giving future generations of redwoods the resources to thrive. That is how it's been for millions of years. Such everlasting endurance is a testament to the resilience of life. So let us accept the truths revealed by the redwood, and like it, learn to harness the gifts of strength within us."

Maral lowered her head in humility before the redwood but quickly lifted it again, her brow furrowed. "Strength? Does it mean to overpower another, like the dawn conquers the night?"

Bilge opened his eyes wider. "No, my friend. Strength and overpowering are never equal. Unlike the interplay of night and day, to compel an unwilling creature is an action taken by the weak, by those lacking the humility and knowledge required to persuade with gentle command. It is unwise to attempt to force another living being to do as you wish. To impose *your* will on a being endowed with its *own* will is to fail to respect the very core of its being."

Looking downward, he shook his head. "Never force."

"If force isn't strength, then what is?" asked the fawn.

"Strength comes from respecting life. Inner strength is acknowledging that every participant in life has its own endless stream of wishes, goals—and choices to make. Dignity is a birthright, but it's lost if we do not have the privilege to make our own choices. Life is an awe-inspiring, though short-lived, gift from the eternal heavens. Regard all life, Maral, and you will know what it is to possess strength."

"Just like the redwood!" squealed Maral. "It is strong yet gentle."

"Right you are," replied Bilge. "The redwood, being among the strongest and mightiest of nature's creations, has never hurt a fly."

For a moment, Maral beamed even brighter than the gnome's lantern.

In reverence, the gnome patted the massive, thick trunk of the redwood. Then he looked down to where the trunk joined the earth. "Strong as it is, a tree over a thousand years old is still bound to the ground by its roots."

"The redwood is grounded," said Maral in jest.

"You are not wrong, Maral," the gnome replied with utmost seriousness. "Like all trees artfully crafted by nature's careful hands, the redwood, too, is grounded in its own strength. Over the years, the redwood learns to know itself deeply. This knowledge helps it skillfully navigate the society of trees competing for resources—and thrive."

With that, Bilge moved onward. Close behind, Maral stumbled across the knotty tree roots pushing up from the forest floor.

3
BE LIKE THE WILDFLOWER

*T*he forest's earthy scents permeated the air the gnome and the fawn breathed as they walked. Spotty white mushrooms cozily poked out of the soft ground. Every few seconds, the brilliant blues and yellows of birds in flight flickered against the forest's camouflaging shades of greens and browns.

"While having roots is important, the freest of forest life also offers gems of wisdom," the gnome said to his youthful companion.

Bilge directed the glow of his lantern toward a burst of color in the dark soil. He shuffled closer to it, and Maral followed. "Here's a reminder from a wildflower."

A tender green stem pushed through the forest floor. From within the plant, a flower with two layers of red and yellow petals blossomed.

"It looks like a glorious star," said Maral. "What does it remind us of?"

The gnome smiled. "It inspires us to be like it, be like the wildflower: wild and free."

Maral blinked. Her reflective black eyes sparkled as the light of the lantern danced across them.

"Freedom," said the gnome, caressing his long white beard, "is a privilege for all life to enjoy—humans, animals, and plants. All life. How does a living creature keep its dignity if it does not live as it chooses? When life gives us freedom, this freedom gives us life."

"To be free is to do whatever we want," said Maral as her chest puffed up proudly.

Shaking his head and his thinning beard, the gnome countered his friend's reasoning. "To be free is to do the *right* thing. Only by knowing and doing what is right can we align with our truest nature."

The fawn was quick to respond. "But we all make mistakes. And some of us, though we know what is right, we do the wrong thing anyway."

Bilge laughed. "You are perceptive, my friend. But I must correct you: Those who do what is wrong do not truly know what is right. The innermost nature of all living creatures answers to a higher purpose—which always stands with what is good and true."

Along the unworn path grew several clusters of brilliant, cheerful wildflowers.

Bilge stooped and, without uprooting the flower from its home in the earth, carefully held the soft, delicate petals between his fingers. "In a sense, we are all born free—free to enjoy life's refreshing gifts of bounty, free to be who we are, free to express our innermost sentiments."

Maral interrupted with passion in her voice, her back stiffened in defiance. "Some of us are not so lucky, like the animals who are captured by the hard-hearted and chained up all their lives. The chained and the caged are not free."

The gnome frowned. "Sadly, no, they are not, at least not in the worldly sense. Indeed, animals chained to a tree do not experience physical freedoms. But for the brave, their spirits are not defeated." Misty-eyed, he stared off into the mysterious depths of the forest beyond the darkened thickets.

"Those captured exchange freedom for reliable food, water, and warmth—but the trade-off is not their choice. It is their unfortunate fate to never know the nectar of freedom that wild forest creatures enjoy, the bliss of exploring the endless expanses of wild terrain that the earth has to offer, the joy of feeling the untamed breeze run through their fur, and the rapture of simply experiencing the kind of dignity that is only present in those who know true liberty."

"Life must be easy for them, though," said the fawn thoughtfully. "They don't need to hunt or forage for food."

Bilge looked into the dark eyes of his protégé and gave her a firm but gentle reminder: "Life is easy for no one, Maral. Anything alive deserves our respect."

The gnome released from his fingers the petals he had carefully held just moments before, leaving the wildflower to continue flourishing in the soil.

4
BE LIKE THE FERN

*T*he pair continued their journey through the forest. Every now and then, the gnome switched his lantern from one hand to the other.

The demure flame produced a far more expansive light than would be expected. The little yellow fire danced as the wind blew effortlessly through the complex maze of intertwined tree trunks growing freely in the forest soil.

The peaceful silence was broken by the gnome's next lesson. "Remember, Maral, that at various times in life, nature teaches you to draw upon different strengths."

Hovering his lantern over a slender, elegant plant protruding from the ground, the gnome said, "Take the fern, for example."

Bilge and Maral watched as the fern gently arched its graceful stems and long leaves in the cool morning breeze. "See the carefree way it bends?"

"Yes," said Maral. "The stems are limber."

"Right. And like the other plants, the fern has something to say."

"Could you tell me what?"

Bilge gazed, enchanted, at the dainty and perfect curves of the fern's stems. After several seconds of silent admiration, he shook himself out of his daze. "Of course. I was wrapped up in esteem for this exquisite fern. But I've gathered my wits about me." He cleared his throat. "Now where was I?"

"What the fern has to say," said Maral.

"Ah yes."

The gnome's lantern swayed in the breeze. As the fern's leaves bent against the wind, he said, "Be like the fern: bendable and yielding."

"Must I always be bendable and yielding?" asked Maral.

"Oh no." The gnome shook his head. "Yield when the time is right to yield. Be strong, like the redwood, when it is time to be strong."

"So," said Maral, whose confidence was growing, "yield with strength."

The gnome laughed, as would a proud father. "You're catching on, my dear!"

16

"Does it mean I'm weak if I'm flexible, though?"

The gnome answered by asking another question. "Does the fern break when it bends?"

"No, the fern stays nimble."

"Right you are. If the fern were stiff, a simple breeze would snap it in half instantly. The poor thing would be utterly broken. But by being 'bendable,' or 'flexible' as you say, the fern temporarily alters its direction and stays intact and well-off."

Maral nodded. "Yes, staying well is all well and good."

The gnome chuckled.

"Let's continue our walk. The fiery sun is rising over the treetops. We shall reach the end of the forest and make our way back by evening, I'm sure."

Beneath the canopies of trees, darkness still engulfed the deep forest. The gnome's lantern helped light the way.

Its wick would last just a day.

5
BE LIKE THE SAP OF THE MAPLE TREE

"*I* could use a snack," said the gnome, as they moved on. He reached into his pocket and pulled out a tidbit in the shape of a maple leaf. "Would you like a bit of maple candy?"

Bilge held out his palm to Maral. In it lay a tan-colored candy. The fawn took a bite of the treat, and the gnome gobbled up the rest.

Chomping as they walked, the gnome said to Maral, "Tasty, isn't it? I made it myself from the sap of the maple tree. Where, oh where?" The gnome stopped beside a leafy tree and directed the light of the lantern to its bark. "Ah, now, here we are—just what I'd been looking for."

Looking up toward the treetops, the gnome said, "This, dear Maral, is the maple tree, from which maple syrup comes."

"What can we learn from the maple tree?" asked Maral.

"Oh, there is much to learn, without a doubt." Still chewing, the gnome looked down at his beard. Crumbs had gathered in it, and he brushed them away. "Can get messy sometimes."

Maral ducked her head and laughed.

"Lesson, now, let's see," he said, finishing his candy. "Of course, Maral. Be like the sap of the maple tree: abundant and sweet."

"I like that one!"

"It suits you just fine, being as sweet as you are!" said the gnome with a chuckle. "The maple tree gives us gallons of sweet sap, enough to make dozens of batches of delightful maple candies."

Bilge rubbed his chin and thought out loud. "I must remember to make twice as many candies as I usually do. My stash runs out more quickly every time. I enjoy the candies too much—and perhaps a little too often!"

"How do you make them?" asked Maral.

"I'm more than happy to show you, my friend!" The gnome inched toward the trunk of the maple tree. "I tap the maple tree to collect the sap. But before that, I find a fir. I need a small piece of its fine wood."

The gnome looked around the forest. "Here, like this." He broke off a small branch of a fir tree, then patted the pockets of his jacket. "Now, where is my carving knife? Ah, here it is." He produced a sharp metal blade.

"Such a perfect tool for forest life. I whittle the wood until I create a spile, like this," said the gnome, showing his creation to Maral.

He then brought out another tool from his pockets and bore a hole in the maple tree. "Next, I insert the spile."

A few drops of maple sap, clear as fresh water, started to trickle down the spile. "Unfortunately, we don't have a bucket on us to catch the sap. Some days it pours like a river. Other days, only a trickle comes out."

"When the sap pours like a river, it's abundant!"

"Quite right, Maral. The sap of the maple tree feeds not only me but also the woodpeckers of the forest. The birds peck a hole in the tree and savor the tasty drink."

He grinned. "But that's just the start of this delicious process! Next, I must light my fire-pit and boil the sap until it transforms into rich, golden maple syrup."

"And maple syrup becomes maple candy!" exclaimed Maral.

"Not instantly. I must add one simple ingredient: butter. That's what we just nibbled on," said Bilge. "Maple syrup whipped up with butter."

Maral licked a crumb from the edge of her mouth and smiled.

"Now I must plug this hole to protect the tree from insects," said the gnome. He shuffled over the forest ground, looked around at the nearby trees, and then picked up an oak branch.

As he carved the branch into a plug for the hole, he said, "Let's return to the lessons the sap of the maple gives us."

"I'm listening," said Maral.

"As I said, we must be like the sap of the maple tree."

"It's sweet!"

"Quite right. Be as sweet as the maple sap but not any sweeter. By being too sweet, you lose yourself, and you never want to lose yourself."

"Oh no, I sure don't," said the fawn, shaking her head.

"Now, bona fide kindness, or sweetness, call it what you will, comes from the right place. Kindness must be genuine; otherwise, it's as useless as a broken door. A broken door will swing back and hit you in the face."

"Huh?" asked Maral, her expression full of bewilderment.

"Sweetness from an impure place is nothing but weakness. Kindness requires inner strength and selfless intentions—and the intended recipient is sure to instantly detect both. If the wily coyote were to give you a piece of good advice, would you take it?"

Maral took a step back and wiggled her brown head. "Why, no. I wouldn't trust it!"

"But if I gave you the exact same piece of good advice, would you be more likely to accept it?"

The fawn smiled and nodded emphatically. "Yes, certainly!"

The gnome inhaled the earthy forest air through his large nostrils and said in a comforting tone, "The quality of kindness depends on the giver. In any case, genuine sweetness is always appreciated."

"Of course it is!" said the fawn. "I appreciate *your* genuine kindness."

"I'm glad you do. But," said the gnome, as he waved his index finger, "in order to give authentic kindness, one must have it within oneself to give. Consider that an empty teapot has nothing to pour out of its spout—the teapot is simply a shiny adornment—but a full teapot satisfies by pouring forth many cups of simmering hot tea. True kindness requires you to have much of yourself to give."

Bilge plugged the hole in the tree. Hobbling along, the gnome continued, "And to have much of yourself to give, you must first be kind to yourself."

"But thinking of myself is selfish, isn't it?"

The gnome laughed and shook his head. "My little one, you misunderstand. It is foolish to not be kind to oneself first. If I neglected to feed myself, I'd have no energy to devote to feeding others. If I hurried to serve others when I required rest, I'd be too worn to offer decent services.

A wise creature knows the importance of being kind to oneself *before* being kind to others."

Speaking confidently, Bilge said, "You are a living being like all others, Maral, and deserve your own sweet care."

A peaceful expression spread across the fawn's countenance.

Then, abruptly, she tilted her head. "Is insincere kindness possible?"

The gnome looked puzzled for a moment.

"I wouldn't call it insincere kindness." He paused. "Or I might, I don't know. But trying too hard to win over others is off-putting, just as an overly sweetened piece of maple candy is sickening rather than pleasing."

The gnome looked into Maral's attentive face with serenity. "Just remember, authentic kindness, which always comes from a place of wisdom, will never steer you in the wrong direction."

6
BE LIKE THE VIOLET

The fawn and gnome walked on, crunching over dead leaves. Hummingbirds of all varieties sang with staccato chirps. With a smile on his face, Bilge enjoyed the sounds of his feathered friends' cheerful songs, and Maral glanced up to catch the shimmery colors of their flitting wings. As she did, her hoof stomped on a violet growing below her.

The observant gnome stopped, pointed to the dainty flower, and said, "Your hoof crushes the tender violet."

Maral lifted her hoof, stepped back, and looked at the smashed flower. "I meant no harm!" said the fawn, looking horrified. Her confidence took a tumble, and she began to shake.

"Ah, not to worry. It is all in the circle of life, Maral. None of us can escape the birth and end of life, not even the stars twinkling beyond the treetops. Yet the forest shows us another secret to a happy life."

Bilge patted Maral on the head and bent down to pick up the crumpled violet. Holding it between his pudgy fingers, he said quietly, "Be like the violet: humble and forgiving."

Noticing Maral's quivering legs, the gnome said, "It is as important to forgive oneself as it is to forgive others."

The fawn lowered her head. "I'll try."

"Forgiveness, of yourself or others, might happen in a blissful second, Maral, or it can take persistent effort over an unimaginable length of time—it can be that difficult. The road to forgiveness has been known to be long."

"But forgiveness, being such a worthwhile virtue, should be easy! Forgiveness is good for everyone."

The wise gnome, still holding the crushed violet, looked at the flower and then back at Maral. "Try as we might, we can never fool ourselves or others when it comes to this most benevolent of acts," he said gently. "Forgiveness, my dear friend, can never be counterfeited. Mercy is a genuine awakening of the slumbering heart, the courage of a heart that has hidden itself to evade another hurt. Mercy requires courage."

Maral's ears perked up. "Why does forgiveness take courage?"

"The practice of all forms of beneficence requires this most fundamental virtue," Bilge replied. "Rather than cower behind the fear of being hurt further, one summons the courage to overcome that fear and deliver compassion to the wrongdoer. In the eyes of the offended, does the wrongdoer deserve mercy? Sometimes not, and this is what makes forgiveness incredibly difficult.

"But being given life by the universe, we are all deserving of clemency. Likewise, as naturally valuable parts of the universe, all beings are gifted with the potential for that courage." Bilge carefully placed the crushed violet back on the ground to rest. "But remember, forgiveness takes its own time."

"Really?" asked the fawn. "But I'd rather forgive right away!"

"Oftentimes you can, and it's wonderful to forgive and forget," said the gnome with a compassionate smile. "But sometimes forgiveness can take a lifetime."

"A lifetime?" Maral exclaimed. "What if a creature lives only a few years?"

"Or a few days," retorted the gnome, "like that fragile violet. Every living thing, no matter how long its life span, has within its grasp the courage to forgive—that selfless heart is what differentiates the living from the unliving."

The fawn tilted her head. Her eyes shone brightly.

"There's a question behind your sparkling eyes, I presume?" asked Bilge as he looked at Maral, sensing the fawn was thirsty for knowledge.

"Yes, there is. What if a creature were to live a hundred years?"

Understanding the heart of his friend, the gnome responded with another question, "Like a human?"

Maral nodded emphatically.

The gnome exhaled and looked up at the sky through the thick canopy of trees. "One of the blessings of being human is having the capacity for patience. And patience is a prerequisite for genuine forgiveness."

The curious fawn gazed at her friend as he spoke.

"Deep hurt requires a profound searching of the heart. So true forgiveness, Maral, happens over time. You cannot ask the sun to rise any faster than it does. Yet, when the heavenly sphere patiently makes its way up into the sky, it is one of the most glorious things to behold here on earth. Likewise, forgiveness is the magnificent rising of the humble heart. And those are privileged who experience either."

The beginnings of daybreak gradually spread across the morning sky above the forest. Thin beams of light penetrated the treetops and brightened miniature slivers of the forest floor. The gnome and the fawn basked in a slender ray of sunlight as they held their thoughtful conversation.

"For all your life, there will be much to forgive," Bilge continued. "It's best to start practicing forgiveness now. Given the nature of our world and all that is contained within it, you will surely have a need for it. As long as the breath of life flows through you, there will be a need for forgiveness. And for your efforts, Maral, forgiveness will reward you with the sweet freedom of peace."

Through the overgrown forest, the gnome and his young student resumed their journey.

Maral was silent for some time.

"You seem steeped in thought, Maral," said the gnome. "What is it you feel?"

"I feel inspired."

"It is quite right to feel inspired by the gifts of humanity."

"These are the gifts of humanity?" asked the fawn, as her eyes widened.

"Indeed, they are," said the gnome. "Strength, freedom, yielding, sweetness, and forgiveness—these are some of the qualities that bring out the best in humanity. Accept the truths told by the forest and you will feel the happiness of humankind. But there is much more to learn. Follow me."

As they trampled over the knotted tree roots jutting out from the ground and the prickly pine needles covering the forest floor, the gnome heard fallen twigs crack and dried leaves steadily rustle in front of them.

"Wait!" he said, holding up his palm. "What are those sounds? It seems, Maral, we are not alone."

"I don't hear anything," said Maral loudly.

"Shh. I hear a slithering. Quick, behind this bush."

Bilge and Maral darted for cover and listened, crouching. Peeking out his head from behind the bush, the gnome peered into the dimness of the forest. "I see its long, dark body. It is a boa constrictor. We must be careful, Maral."

"We must be strong," whispered Maral. "Let's stomp it out!"

"No, no, Maral!" Bilge replied with urgency. "We're no match for that serpent. It will squeeze us to a pulp and swallow the both of us whole. It is useless to fight force with force. Now is a time to yield. Let it pass. Be still."

Both the gnome and the fawn remained low behind the bush and waited. Maral's legs quivered despite her efforts to remain still, while the gnome crouched motionlessly. With attentive ears, he listened for signs that the snake had passed.

Minutes later, Bilge peeped over the top of the bushes to scan their immediate environment. "Ah, the coast is clear, Maral. The serpent has moved on."

Maral hopped up onto her four legs and leaped out of the bush, regaining her composure, while Bilge breathed a sigh of relief.

As the two marched on, the gnome sung to himself, "There is a time to yield and a time to be strong. There is a time for quiet and a time for song . . ."

Maral listened to her wise friend with a smile.

7
BE LIKE THE DAMAGED SILVER MAPLE

*O*nce the two had made some headway through the tangled forest, the gnome stopped before a tree revealing its profound natural truths.

"Ah, what have we here? Poor thing." The gnome grazed the trunk with his palm. "Do you see this bulge on the silver maple?"

Maral nodded. "It's just a bump. I sort of like it."

"It appears as just a bump to us, but it causes the tree incredible suffering. The unusual formation is called a burl. No one knows exactly why some trees develop burls and others do not. It is a mystery of life. Perhaps insects damaged this bark, or the tree is responding to some other wound. Regardless, the burl is lifelong damage. It will continue to grow for as long as the tree lives. The tree will bear an extra burden all its life."

"What does the burl do to the tree?" asked Maral.

Bilge looked the tree up and down. "Well, it diminishes the tree's health, and with a burl like this, the tree may not have long to live."

The fawn frowned. "I still don't understand. It's just a bulge. I see nothing wrong with it."

"You are one of a kind, Maral." He glanced at the fawn with a tender smile, then patted the trunk of the tree and continued, "Despite this flaw, the silver maple remains a valuable part of the forest ecosystem and is as worthy of dignity as any other life form on earth. Forest birds build nests in the highest treetops. The silver maple leaves provide shade to weary animals who scamper underneath it after a day in the sun. The branches are a playground for squirrels."

"The burl is just a small part of the tree," said Maral, observing the formation.

"Maral, your kind heart sees deeply. There is much more to the innocent tree than this burl. It possesses a complete identity."

The gnome tenderly touched the burl again. "Only a small part of this magnificent silver maple is damaged. As you can see, the rest of the tree thrives: the hardy branches, the tender green stems, the leaves with healthy veins pumping nutrients through them, and the robust trunk that serves as the base for its very life. A precious thing of life should never be judged based on its flaws alone. Plus, had we not come across this damage, the silver maple's burl, we'd never have had the good fortune to discover the formative truths it has to offer."

"What does the silver maple offer us?" asked Maral.

"Pay close attention. With the burl on its trunk, this silver maple is unlike most other trees in the forest. Yet its unusualness does not prevent the tree from enjoying the life it has been given. The silver maple wisely embraces its flaw. Mustering all its courage and inner strength, the tree pushes beyond the pain and even flourishes."

Inspired by the tree's resilience, Bilge joyfully continued, "Despite its damage, the tree contributes beauty to the world. See how its leaves playfully dance under the sunlight? The woodpeckers of our forest are drawn to the unique swirling grain patterns found nowhere else but within the burls. When the birds peck into the trunk to build homes, they create some of the most decorative residences in the forest. There is a dignified graciousness in this silver maple, Maral. I encourage you to be like the damaged silver maple: accepting of self and flourishing.

"Do I have flaws?" asked Maral.

The gnome laughed. "Yes, you and I both. You, for instance, muster the strength to push beyond the doubts that hold you back. Your flaws become tiny when you summon the might and will to overcome them. You have already shown growth by bravely facing your weaknesses. A flaw is not always unwelcomed, especially when it is utilized as a stepping-stone toward perfection. Just remember, every one of us has flaws. That is the nature of life. But to me, Maral, you are perfect."

8
BE LIKE THE ACORN

*T*wo squirrels ran past the fawn and the gnome. "Little critters are always busy," said Bilge with a chuckle, as he eyed the animals chasing each other up and down tree trunks. "Never a dull moment for squirrels, not in this natural playground. They will soon be looking for food to prepare for the winter."

Spying something small and brown and fashioned with a tan cap, Bilge bent down to pick it up from the ground. "What have we here? It is none other than the tiny seed of the grand oak tree." He showed the acorn to Maral. "These are what the squirrels store away to help them survive the long cold months."

Maral playfully pushed the acorn with her nose. "It is so small. What grand truth could it possibly hold?"

"A truth that applies to all living creatures on earth," he said. "Be like the acorn: a small part of something bigger." Still gazing at the seed, Bilge said to Maral, "You, too, are like the acorn."

"Me?" said the fawn with a squeal, as she playfully trotted a few steps back. "How so?"

"All of life has a place in this world. Even the tiniest beings have a role to play in the grand scheme of life, mysterious as that role may seem at first. Without you, I'd not be on this invigorating walk! It does me good to get out of my hut now and then, Maral." The gnome laughed from deep within his round belly and gave it a pat.

Still holding the acorn, the gnome expanded on his comparison: "Do not be fooled by this tiny acorn. What was once tiny becomes gigantic. What seems trivial at first can later become important. A small acorn can lie on the ground with its cap for weeks. But when the conditions are right, and the wind blows it into the rich soil, the acorn that once seemed aimless starts to root and grow. After many years, it becomes a tree—one whose boughs offer shade, whose branches lend the forest birds a place to build their nests, and whose acorns give magnificent life to new oak trees."

Maral bent her head down and rolled an acorn along with her nose. Then she pushed it deeper into the soil.

The gnome watched his friend's compassionate gesture and continued, "Everything, big or small, has a place on this earth, from the drops of rain that land in the rivers and eventually travel to fill the oceans, to the individual grains of rice that grow in plenty and feed entire civilizations."

"There, that acorn should sprout now," said Maral, still peering at the spot where she had just planted the acorn.

"It is good of you, Maral, to see the value of that tiny acorn. In time, you may experience the value the fledgling plant will bring to the world."

Maral beamed and held her head high.

"We don't always recognize the worth of little things at first," said Bilge, "but all of life changes with time."

"Like that acorn! It will grow into a splendid oak tree."

"Yes, from a rolling seed to a tender plant to a fledgling tree to, at last, a majestic oak. We shall not be here to see this little acorn mature to an old oak, but we can hope it will one day reach its full potential."

Maral shifted her gaze from the ground to her friend. "Can you further explain how all of life changes?"

The gnome cleared his throat and blinked. He, too, looked from the ground to his companion.

"Eh? Changes?" He looked toward the heavens, attempting to collect his wandering thoughts. "Ah yes, of course. Sometimes my mind escapes me, being as old as I am, and trying to collect my thoughts is like trying to catch the clouds. Now, let's see, it would help to think of life as the sky." He pointed upward, in the direction of his gaze.

His voice crackling, he said, "Yes, every fleeting moment, the sky changes. Each second, the sky we see presently is a once-in-a-lifetime opportunity. On the sunniest days, like today, the shapes of the clouds grow mightily and then wither pitifully. Even across a thunderous sky, the clouds billow swiftly. No matter who or what tries to stop it, the sky is never the same, not for one second, not ever again for all eternity."

Bilge and Maral peered toward the blue heavens and the cascading cloud formations and stood mesmerized.

The gnome interrupted their shared moment of awe. "Sometimes the sky is beautiful. At other times it is terrifying. The one constant is that the sky is forever in flux—just like life."

He paused and observed his friend. "You may feel unimportant now. But do not count on staying that way, Maral. Life holds great glories for those willing to be patient."

As they resumed their walk, the gnome said, "You will know your destiny, eventually."

Hearing her companion's words, Maral stood a little taller.

9
BE LIKE THE BRISTLECONE PINE

*R*ays of sunlight filtered through the treetops, creating golden kaleidoscopes within the forest's dark recesses, as Maral and Bilge started climbing. The steep, rocky part of the forest was hardly a hurdle for the nimble Maral, but the gnome stopped frequently to catch his breath and rub his sore knees.

"Maral," said Bilge, between long huffs of breath, "my legs are in no shape to climb such heights. Bear with me, and we will eventually make it to the top, where our hard-earned truths will not disappoint."

Maral walked closely beside her white-bearded friend, offering her spotted back as support. The air was drier at the higher elevation. Here, the forest floor was no longer a vibrant, lush carpet of mosses and grasses.

"Hardly anything grows here," said Maral, looking around in surprise at the almost-barren land in a forest normally brimming with trees, shrubs, and greenery.

"Ah, you are right, Maral," said the gnome, gasping for breath. "At this elevation, the land is harsh. Only the toughest of survivors thrive here."

The fawn and gnome gradually made their way to the very top of ten thousand feet of limestone soil. And they found that something grand did grow there, in a place strewn with jagged rocks.

The duo stood under the twisted boughs of a bristlecone pine.

"Look at the winding limbs," said Maral. "I've never seen anything like it."

"Fascinating, isn't it?" said Bilge. "Centuries of mighty winds have shaped these bristlecone pine trees, setting them apart from all other trees on earth."

"And yet, they stand so . . . alone," remarked the fawn.

The gnome nodded. "Ah, yes. This kind of strength is reserved for the few."

"Are we to learn about strength from the bristlecone pine?" asked Maral. "Like we did from the redwood?"

"Certainly, as these trees represent gritty strength—even among the toughest conditions. Their branches proudly reach high into the heavens, despite their roots diving deep into the poorest soil. But we are here to learn something different from this tree, Maral. We are here to learn to be like the bristlecone pine: self-respecting and dignified."

The young fawn's eyebrows arched upward. "Hmm?"

"Maral, the bristlecone pine is no ordinary tree. Over the span of five thousand years, this inspiring life form has seen ice ages and volcanoes and the rise and fall of great civilizations."

Maral gaped. "It's quite an old tree."

"And yet it flourishes alone. Despite being thrashed by ice, wind, and rain, and having the poorest of nutrients to feed on, the bristlecone pine remains triumphant. In the face of eons of adversity, the tree stands with dignity. Every twist of its trunk radiates self-respect. It is a tree I deeply admire."

Maral cocked her head to one side. She gazed with her doe eyes at the delicate twists of the tree trunk.

"I wish for you to experience the dignity of one of the oldest living trees on the planet," said Bilge.

"It has a dignity that comes from naught but within itself." Then the gnome spoke in a hushed voice. "That is where true dignity arises—from within."

Maral was contemplative for some time. She and her companion stood next to each other, innocence and experience, both in awe of the ancient tree with lessons tucked into every nook and twist of its resilient trunk and branches.

"Better come along now," said Bilge, breaking the respectful silence. "It is nearing midday, and we must be back before nightfall, Maral."

Maral blinked, as if to break free of a daze, then began to follow Bilge back down the rocky slope. Before the bristlecone pine was out of sight, she turned to look at it once more. Then she trotted to catch up with the gnome.

"Downhill is always easier, Maral, especially for older folks, like me."

Maral giggled.

"It took some time and effort to climb the slope, Maral, but dignity is worth learning about. Wouldn't you say so? Life loses its meaning without self-respect."

Maral nodded eagerly as she followed her friend.

"Without a truly respectable *me*, there is no truly respectable *us*." Bilge analyzed the downward slope and strategically avoided setting foot on loose rocks.

He continued speaking with labored breathing: "Self-respect is the key to a valuable friendship and even to a civilization's success. Solid relationships and prosperous societies are made up of dignified equals. In order to respect other members of our forest world, we must first respect ourselves. Self-respect is the firm foundation for a good life."

The gnome and the fawn inched down the steep slope, carefully moving along the treacherous route back to the forest floor.

10
BE LIKE THE WIND

*B*ilge was still breathing laboriously as the pair reached the bottom of the slope. When his feet touched flat earth, the gnome twisted the cap off his canteen. He took a big gulp of water. "Would you like some, Maral?"

Maral stretched out her neck. Bilge poured out a stream of water, and the fawn drank. Then the gnome put the cap back on his canteen and smacked his lips.

"Ah! That was refreshing. And we have made it back to solid ground. I'd say it's time to uncover a much easier truth—one that has followed us from the start."

The fawn quivered. "Something has followed us?" In a forest filled with predators, a fawn had to remain vigilant at all times.

"Be at ease, Maral," said Bilge, as he laughed and stroked the fawn's back. "What has followed us is changeable and—"

"A shape-shifter?" Again, the fawn's slender body tensed up. She darted her gaze around the dim environment, looking for hungry creatures that might make an instant meal out of her.

"Be unafraid, Maral. It is only the wind that follows us wherever we go."

Maral let out a loud exhale. Along with it, she released a carton of pent-up fear.

The gnome resumed ambling and bumbling in his customary way.

"The glorious wind leads us and follows us, no matter where we are on earth. The wind carries us forward and pushes us back."

"Whatever for?" asked Maral.

"The wind has its own way of being, just like you and I do. But it delivers an important message every time it passes."

"I've heard the wind carries tales," said the fawn with a nod.

"The wind carries tales, it pushes sails, it whispers, and it howls. The wind is a powerful beast, a steady friend, and a constant companion to all life on earth."

The fawn grinned. "The wind whispers secrets, like a friend."

The gnome laughed. "Ah, you jest, but it is true! The wind crosses the earth, observing all of life as it passes through. In its endless journeys, it witnesses what some would never want revealed to others."

Maral's ears twitched, as if capturing the breeze. "If only the wind had a voice."

"The wind is not without a voice, Maral. At times, the wind does howl—we might say in agony at witnessing what goes on in some parts of our forest realm," replied the gnome, growing somber.

"Like the doings of the *carnavariche* Kotu," said the fawn gravely.

The gnome nodded. "Yes, like the actions of the wicked beast Kotu, of whom even the wind is afraid."

After inhaling the fresh forest air deeply, the gnome said, "The wind is able to cross all parts of the globe because of its distinctive characteristics. It is unlike any other earthly phenomenon."

"What makes the wind so special?" asked Maral.

By now the pair had nearly reached the outermost edges of the forest. Under the leafy treetops, the ground upon which the gnome and fawn walked was shaded. Though it was almost midday, the sun barely had the strength to pierce the flourishing woodland.

The gnome's lantern lit the way.

"If we listen carefully, we will hear how special it is to be like the wind: determined yet adapting. These traits have allowed the wind to remain successful since the beginning of time on earth and beyond."

"Beyond? Do you mean the whole universe?" asked Maral.

"Indeed, Maral. All parts of the universe harbor the wind. Wind blows across the dusty planets near ours, but it is best we focus on our beloved forest here on earth. Wind is the same, no matter what habitat we take up in the universe."

"I'd like for you to say more about the wind," said Maral.

At that moment, a cool breeze fluttered through the gnome's shirt. His sleeves crinkled and his beard briefly fluttered. Bilge closed his eyes and paused to enjoy the sensation.

"It is spontaneous," said the gnome with a smile, his eyes still closed. "The wind comes whenever it wants and offers its satisfying breeze."

Maral stopped to enjoy the breeze too. She closed her eyes and held her head high as the wind blew across her spotted brown fur.

"How does the wind last as long as eternity?"

"Because it is determined," replied Bilge. "And because it is adaptable."

"You see this rock, Maral?" Bilge pointed to a two-foot-high boulder with a crown of grass growing around its edge.

Maral nodded. "Mm-hmm."

"The big rock, though it stands in the way of the wind, is no match for it."

Maral's head tilted to the side, and her eyes became wide. "How so?"

"The wind is determined to follow its course. And to achieve its end, it must be adaptable. And so, when the wind cannot pass through an obstacle in its way, like this rock, it blows over it in a big sweep." He threw his hands in the air, mimicking the course of the wind.

"Yes, that is adaptable."

"You and I are no match for the wind. We stand in its way at times, but the wind has no need to pass through us. It simply blows over or to the sides of us. The wind is clever, no?"

"And yet it goes to wherever it intends," said Maral, now jumping up and down on her light feet, as she understood the wind's ingenuity.

"Adaptable, indeed. Determined, no doubt," said Bilge. "That is how one succeeds."

Only half of the wick remained in the gnome's lantern. "It is high noon, Maral. See, the sun is directly above us. And we are just nearing the edge of the forest."

"Our halfway point?" asked Maral. She leaped joyfully.

"Correct! We have arrived just in time to the forest's edge. Now we simply need to return, circling the other half of the forest, of course, to accomplish our journey. We will be back before nightfall, as planned, before we are at the mercy of the hungry forest creatures that come out to hunt. The forest never sleeps, Maral. We must be careful."

Maral's eyes grew wider, and her slender body trembled.

PART II: THE RETURN JOURNEY

11
AN ENCOUNTER WITH KOTU

The gnome hobbled on, humming a lighthearted tune. With each step, his feet crunched over fallen leaves. As Maral followed, a deep rumble from within the unfathomable depths of the earth shook the ground.

"Oh, oh! What's that, Maral?" Bilge stopped in his tracks and moved his lantern in a rapid circle to reveal what might be lurking within their surroundings.

Another rumble sounded. The noise was like an aching groan coming from the mouth of an empty, hungry cave.

"Perhaps it is just an angry wind," replied Maral.

"Angry it is, whatever it is," said the gnome in a hushed tone, still gazing around. Birds squawked frantically. Leaves rustled violently. The wind howled eerily.

"Shall we continue this way?" asked Maral. She hopped forward a few steps. "Or go back?"

Before Bilge could reply, the earth shook with the might of a thousand galloping stallions, and without further warning, cracked open. Maral's hind legs slipped into the ground as it separated, and although she tried desperately to pull herself out, she was no match for the forces of gravity, and fell deep into the cavernous hole. "Help!" she screamed.

"Maral!" shouted the gnome. He stretched out his arm, but the fawn had already been swallowed by the open earth.

As Maral fell, a tree whose roots had been loosened by the tremors also fell with a cacophonous thud across the hole in the earth. The impact released a blinding swirl of dust and dirt.

Then there was silence.

The gnome coughed out the dirt that he'd breathed in and rubbed his eyes to rid them of the dust. He coughed again. "Mar . . . Maral!"

The fawn didn't answer.

"Maral! Are you there? Answer me!" Bilge directed the beam of his lantern into the hole. Still unable to see her, he rubbed his sweaty palms and paced back and forth in short steps. "Oh me, oh my," he said to himself. Again, he peered in.

The gnome heard the crunch of dry leaves coming from the bottom of the hole. "Maral! It was just an earthquake. Maral?"

"I'm here," she replied in a faint voice.

"Are you hurt?" Bilge crouched at the very edge of the gaping hole.

"I think I've been cut," she said weakly.

"You took quite a tumble, and you might have been cut by the branch of the tree trunk as you fell. We must hurry and get you out of there."

"But how?"

As the gnome looked around for a solution, his gaze locked on a pair of penetrating yellow eyes staring out from the bushes on the opposite side of the hole. The bright eyes squinted. Gripped with fear, Bilge stood motionless. Half an eternity seemed to pass in that moment.

"Maral," he said, his voice shaking, "we've got company. It seems the smell of fresh blood from your cut has attracted a creature of the dark."

The carnavariche slowly emerged from the shadow of the bushes. Its intense gaze shifted from the gnome to the trapped fawn. The grayish beast methodically marched on its four legs along the edge of the hole. Salivating, the carnavariche's tongue hung loosely out of its mouth—a mouth filled with two dozen razor-sharp fangs, the longest spanning four inches. Its eyes never left the vulnerable young fawn at the bottom of the hole.

The gnome also paced and scratched his head. "Oh me, oh my," he mumbled. Knowing he must pull himself together quickly, he took a deep breath and assessed the situation—the hole, the fallen tree, the carnavariche, and Maral.

"Ah! Maral, the fallen tree across the hole!" Bilge yelled. "It is your lifeline! Use the very thing that hurt you to your advantage. Quickly, Maral!"

"But how? The fallen trunk is so high!"

"This is no time to doubt!"

The carnavariche stopped and then made a giant leap—into the hole.

"Now, Maral!" the gnome shouted.

Maral took two steps back. Using the strength of her hind legs, she leaped higher than she'd ever leaped in her life. Her forelegs landed on the tree trunk spanning the top of the hole, and she scrambled up. Once all four legs were on the tree, she sprinted to the edge of the hole, and used the full force of her might to kick the tree down into it.

It fell with a crash, and the carnavariche suddenly had no means of escape.

Maral and the gnome sped away from the hole and the beast trapped inside it. Upon reaching a safe spot within the bushes, the gnome, panting, said, "You are safe now, Maral. I did not dare tell you before, as I was afraid you might freeze in fear, but I shall tell you now—the creature we encountered was none other than the most sinister carnavariche of the forest kingdom: Kotu."

Maral's eyes widened. "Kotu! I've never seen him, but the other animals say with shuddering voices that the carnavariche is incredibly evil."

"Eh! *Evil* is a mild term to describe Kotu. He is a powerful force of darkness. Kotu destroys without mercy. And not just bodies. He also ravages souls."

Maral, staggering slightly, stopped in her tracks and turned to face the gnome. "The soul? But the soul goes on forever."

"Yes, the soul is immortal. Indeed, the soul cannot be fully destroyed. But it can become sullied to the point where a creature is no longer certain if it has one—yet it is always there."

Bilge scratched his white beard and looked up, as if questioning the heavens directly. "I've never seen a soul, Maral—only felt it within. It is eternal light. It is wholeness, purity, and everlasting goodness. The soul is a connection to the divine. In fact, the soul is a small part of the divine with which living beings are gifted."

"Do we all have a soul?" asked Maral with innocent eyes.

The gnome nodded almost imperceptibly while remaining steeped in thought. "We all have a soul."

"Even Kotu?" asked the fawn.

The gnome looked directly at Maral. "Even Kotu. But the light of his soul has been darkened by his malicious intentions. The brutal carnavariche no longer listens to the light of goodness within himself, a light that is present within all of life. Kotu purposely walks the long and treacherous path of evil."

With a sigh, Bilge continued, "But Kotu is not one hundred percent evil. If he were, his evil would bring an end to his very being—pure evil is utterly destructive and thereby would destroy even itself."

Maral similarly let out a sigh. "How awful, to have a soul and yet refuse it."

The howl of the lonesome carnavariche trapped in the hole pierced the forest air. Maral's ears were pointed outward on high alert, and her body trembled.

Bilge spoke again, this time in a whisper. "In my many years of life, Maral, I've seen how vicious Kotu can be and the lifelong suffering he has inflicted on innocent creatures. After an animal has been in the carnavariche's grips—if it manages to escape—that animal is never the same wholesome soul. Rather, the poor thing returns to life damaged and miserable. So when a beast like Kotu pounces on his victim, it is my humble belief that even the immortal light of that being's soul dims, until the soul is able to heal. Kotu's evil is that great."

A frown turned Maral's usually gentle expression into a worried one. She searched the forest floor with her downcast eyes, as if seeking out some goodness that could overcome such an evil as she'd just met.

"The destructive power of evil is immense. Unfortunately, evil is intertwined with life on our earthly sphere. There is no fully escaping it . . ." The gnome's voice trailed off softly, and he looked out into the forest realm, where Kotu would remain forever lost in the earth's depths.

Maral hopped next to her friend and, with hope in her voice, comforted the gnome. "There must be something that can be done. Perhaps, like the wind, we can be adaptable, passing around all that evil."

Bilge's gaze returned from far off to focus on the fawn. He breathed out a sigh, and the edges of his wrinkled mouth turned gently upward. "Maral, my optimistic little friend, yes, we can be like the wind and circumvent evil. But there is further hope."

The gnome stroked Maral's head. "You see, great evil requires even greater good to overcome it. You are that greater good, Maral. By mustering strength that you never knew you had, you kicked the tree trunk into the depths of that cavernous pit. Kotu cannot escape—now or ever. He is done for, thanks mostly to you. A sense of serenity can now return to the forest, a peace that has been long overdue. The fearful forest creatures whose lives were shattered by Kotu will start on a long-awaited journey toward healing."

The fawn's worried expression turned to one of glee. Her face lit up like the noonday sun. In little hoppity hops, made smaller by the pain from her wound, she danced around the gnome.

"Given the combination of circumstances—the earthquake, the might of your strength, your innate goodness, and your quick thinking—the forest creatures are safe from Kotu. But naturally, in our world, there will always be other threats that lie in wait.

"Now, let me see your wound, Maral."

The fawn stood still enough to allow the gnome to gently separate her fur and examine her skin. It didn't take long for him to find a cut spanning several inches along her back.

"Nothing a little antiseptic won't heal," he said. Bilge gathered a few medicinal plants from the bushes nearby, crushed the leaves, and applied the healing gel to the wound.

"That should make it better," he said with a smile.

"It feels much better, thank you," said Maral.

"Maral, I must point out that despite having nearly become another victim of the most vicious beast in the forest, you have not given in to bitterness. It seems you have somewhat forgiven your would-be attacker. Forgiveness is a means of escape from the merciless clutches of bitterness."

The fawn was silent, absorbed in her thoughts.
"Um, I've been trying to be like the violet: humble and forgiving," she answered with a smile and a glance toward her friend.

"Indeed, you are like the violet—and like the acorn," said Bilge proudly.

"The acorn? How so?"

"Maral, my friend, as I'd mentioned before, you are like the acorn, a small part of something bigger. Even as you try to forgive, your mercy, too, is a small part of something bigger."

"What is that bigger something?"

"A part of the highest principles of life." Gazing ahead, Bilge absentmindedly caressed his beard, and the two pushed onward.

"That was quite an unexpected ordeal," blurted the gnome after a few minutes of stumbling over mangled tree roots jutting haphazardly out of the ground. In relief, he exhaled loudly. "Though most ordeals are. One thing is clear: the dual powers of nature should be respected. Nature has the might to injure. Nature is also known to heal. Nature can destroy you, and it can uplift you. It is a force to be reckoned with."

Despite being shaken up by the fright of their lives, the gnome and fawn gathered their wits about them and slowly continued their journey.

For a while, their travels were quiet. Even the bravest of souls require moments to reflect on and feel gratitude for having escaped a horrendous, nearly life-changing event.

And then, under the calm of the afternoon sun, Bilge put his arm over Maral's neck and said, "I have never seen you jump so high."

The fawn smiled and said, "I never knew I could jump so high."

12
BE LIKE THE BARK OF THE PINE

The gnome looked up at the sky and pointed. "See the sun, Maral? It is sinking slightly to the west. This means we are a bit beyond the halfway point of our journey. We are circling back around to parts of the forest we've not yet touched."

"We're going home," said Maral.

"We are indeed on our way home, Maral. But the forest still has many truths to reveal—truths that will aid us in our quest for a good, happy life. We shall continue to learn, even as we head back. Nature always has something important to say."

The pair trudged through thick piles of decaying leaves bunched up on the forest floor. The gnome's lantern swayed with each step; its light caught a crack stretching from the uppermost part to the bottom of a tree.

"Ah, see here, Maral. The bark of this pine tree is split open," said the gnome. He brought his lantern closer to the injured tree. The bark's delicate inner layers were exposed.

Bilge and Maral stepped closer to examine it.

"How did such a scar come to be?" asked the fawn.

"It looks like the work of lightning. Lightning strikes about one hundred times every second in our world, and this tall pine tree has been a victim of its fiery temper."

The gnome grazed the damaged trunk. "Poor thing has suffered enormous stress. Yet it still lives."

"I suppose a lightning strike could kill."

"Half of all trees struck by lightning die, Maral. It is a fact. But this pine tree is a survivor, like you. I dare say you have learned to be like the bark of the pine: hardy and brave."

The fawn glanced around at the long scar on her back.

"You showed great resilience and bravery, Maral. Despite your injury, you used your wits to escape the close encounter with the most dangerous predator in the forest."

Maral inhaled the fresh air and filled her lungs. "I feel brave," she said, "and glad."

Bilge laughed, and his bushy white eyebrows bounced. "Certainly, you must be glad to have had the chance to display your bravery, to feel that you have within you an acceptance of the challenges of the forest. I am glad you showed your strength, Maral, but I was frightened. You showed not only yourself but also me the breadth of your courage."

The gnome took out his canteen, unscrewed the cap, and poured what was left of the water into the roots of the tree. "Here you go, pine tree. Your scar needs this water far more than we do in order to heal."

Bilge turned to look at the fawn. "Your physical wounds will heal, too, Maral. It is the pain inside you that I still worry about."

A small smile appeared on Maral's tender face. "As you said, forgiveness offers the gifts of peace and freedom. Don't worry. As you thought before, I *have* been practicing forgiveness all along for my own sake. And I've been rewarded: I feel more at peace."

Bilge, understanding his friend, said, "It takes a great deal of humility to forgive, and now I have no doubt that your humble heart beats strong and free."

In accord, the like-minded friends smiled at each other.

13
BE LIKE THE SYCAMORE SEED

$\mathcal{T}$he two walked on, continuing where no path lay. In
this part of the forest, the sun's rays shone through without
being obstructed by trees, but some areas were lit only by
the gnome's trusty lantern, despite it being early afternoon.

An unusually large shady spot caused the gnome to
pause. He looked up. Above him were the branches of an
enormous tree. Its trunk measured ten feet in diameter, and
its bark had a camouflage pattern—dark brown bark peeled
off in patches to reveal white underneath.

A squirrel sped across the gnome's path and darted into
a hollow in the patchy tree trunk. Maral giggled as she
watched a second rodent try to carry a large store of nuts
in its paws across the forest floor. A few nuts slipped, but

the squirrel speedily picked them up. Alternately dropping and carrying the nuts, the squirrel created quite an amusing scene.

Bilge, still gazing toward the heavens, said, "It must be at least one hundred feet high and its branches equally wide."

The fawn looked away from her entertainment on the forest floor to gaze up as well. "What's one hundred feet high and wide?"

"None other than the marvelous sycamore tree," said Bilge. He reached up and plucked a round hairy ball from its branches.

"A fruit? Can we eat it? I'm starving."

"This is hardly an edible fruit, Maral. What I have in my hands is the hairy-tufted seed of the sycamore tree. The seed head has turned brown, making it much easier to pluck off the branches."

Bilge dug into his jacket pocket. "As for food, Maral, surely I'm either carrying some tidbits, or we shall find something to eat within the natural abundance of our forest."

He spent some time searching his pockets for edibles. "No, no. I believe we've eaten the last maple candies I brought along for our trip. My friend, we shall stumble across something to eat before nightfall."

With her doe eyes, Maral peered at the brown ball the gnome held in his outstretched palm. "What an unusual-looking seed."

"It is a small handful, yet will eventually grow to the wondrous heights of this very sycamore tree."

Bilge looked at Maral. "I dare say, Maral, there is something tiny within you that is growing mighty, like the sycamore tree seed."

The fawn tilted her head, and her sparkling black eyes grew big. She fluttered her long lashes.

"I shan't grow to be as tall as the sycamore tree!" said Maral. She laughed and playfully kicked a few fallen leaves at the gnome's feet.

"Not as tall," the gnome said with a chuckle, "but you see, Maral, you are growing to be like the sycamore seed: starting tiny yet growing mighty."

He rubbed his long beard. As the gnome affectionately gazed at the fawn, he seemed to be lost in his own world.

Maral nudged his arm with her nose.

The gnome snapped out of his daydream and blinked his eyes thrice. "Oh, what was I saying, Maral?"

"The sycamore tree seed."

"Oh, yes, yes. Here in the palm of my hand is the sycamore seed. And it will develop into the great spectacle of might and power that stands before us now." He pointed to the colossal branches of the mature tree.

"This sycamore tree belongs in the wild freedom of the forest, where it has the space to blossom to its fullest potential. It is too grand to grow within the limits of some ordinary backyard. It is meant for bigger things." Bilge looked at Maral and smiled, the wrinkles at the edges of his eyes becoming more distinct.

"But might and power are not everything," said the gnome. "Come along now."

14
BE LIKE THE WEEPING WILLOW

*B*ilge crossed over a bed of rocks at the bottom
of a trickling stream that once gushed with water and
followed the channel. The tiny rivulet widened as he made
strides. Although her wound limited the comfort of her
movements, Maral still managed to play, hopping over the
bubbling water.

"See here, Maral." The gnome pointed. "This small
stream will be joined by other tributaries. Together, they
will lead us to the main river that passes through our forest.
I am expecting that we will stumble upon a small pond
of sorts—one surrounded by trees that hold important
wisdom."

Bilge had walked only a few feet when he glimpsed the graceful branches of weeping willow trees in the distance. The grove surrounded a clear pond. The roots of the weeping willows fed on the pond water.

Maral stopped in her tracks upon seeing the hauntingly beautiful sight. "What elegance! I've never seen such grace in all my life!"

"Indeed, these weeping willow trees are quite a sight. Watch how the curved, hanging branches sway gently in the breeze. They are a thing of natural beauty. And yet, these symbols of new life have much to say."

The fawn stepped closer to the trees, mesmerized. Bilge, too, gazed at the gorgeous grove.

"The curved branches sway nimbly, just like the leaves of the fern. Bendable and yielding—I'm sure that's how they prosper," said the fawn.

"I am sure of it too. Even the strongest of forest animals have a lot to learn from these gentle hulks."

Before the gnome could expand on the lesson, a sudden splashing and squawking pierced the still air. Maral turned to look at the cause of the ruckus. On the opposite side of the pond was a large swan. Her wings flapped as she trumpeted.

"What on earth is that swan doing?" asked Maral.

"I don't know. But we better have a closer look."

The pair walked in the direction of the clatter and splashing.

"Why, it's a cygnet!" said Bilge, pointing to a small bird on the shore. "Look at the baby swan's gray fur. Cute as a button!"

"And frightened," said Maral. "It's so little and utterly confused! But if it is accepting of itself, like the damaged silver maple, it will grow mighty, like the sycamore seed."

"A mighty, beautiful swan," Bilge replied with a wink.

The cygnet waddled back and forth across the edge of the bank. The mother swam closer to her little one. Five other cygnets swam alongside their mother in the pond.

"It seems like this cygnet is too afraid to enter the water!" said Maral.

"It must be her first time swimming."

"And she doesn't know if she can," replied Maral. "I know just how she feels. I, myself, oftentimes don't know if I would ever be able to do things, like leaping out of that deep hole and onto the tree trunk that saved my life."

Bilge looked at Maral with a reassuring smile. "In that instant, you grew mighty."

"I did, like the sycamore seed!"

Maral inched closer to the cygnet scurrying along the bank. The swan flapped her wings and trumpeted loudly as Maral approached the baby.

The sound echoed louder and louder. The cygnet scrambled back and forth even faster.

Maral laughed as the cygnet waddled confusedly. "The water? The ground? Where to?"

"Come on, baby swan," said Bilge. "Into the water you go." He stood on the bank cheering on the cygnet.

Maral took another step toward the cygnet.

"Careful, Maral. The mother swan is very protective. And a swan bite is no laughing matter."

Maral took one more cautious step and gingerly bent her head to the ground. With her nose, she gently nudged the baby swan into the water. As soon as it splashed onto the surface of the pond, the cygnet instinctively paddled its feet and swam toward its awaiting mother. The swan, the cygnet, and its siblings made their way across the pond.

"Look at that happy family," said the gnome. He took his canteen and filled it with the pond water. While doing so, he glanced up at the fawn. "Maral, you certainly have it in you to be like the weeping willow tree: tender and understanding. Even the strongest of forest animals must learn to be gentle as the willow tree—brute force is no match for the strength of a kind heart." The gnome twisted on the cap of his now-full canteen.

"It's nothing," said Maral. "I was a baby once. In many ways, I still am!"

"Aren't we all?" replied Bilge. "I say, there's so much about the natural world that even the oldest of beings have yet to learn." Maral looked at her friend as he stroked his beard. "None of us will ever gain the full knowledge of it. That is the magic and mystery of life."

Maral bounced alongside her friend. "Maybe some of us learn just enough. Just enough to be happy."

"Quite right, quite right. It is the privileged few who are content with their lot."

Then he murmured, "Nature never fails to surprise. There is always something new, always something waiting to be discovered."

Bilge's voice trailed into Maral's ears as he walked on, leading the way. "Never-ending wonders, never-ending delights."

15
BE LIKE THE GINGKO TREE

*M*aral trotted carefully to catch up with Bilge, who was still mumbling to himself and bumbling along. When the fawn's brown coat grazed his sleeve, the gnome snapped out of his conversation with himself.

"Oh! How is your wound, Maral?" asked Bilge. "It pains me to know you've been hurt along our journey. Hopefully the herbal remedy served its purpose and started to heal your injury. It's quite remarkable of you—you haven't complained one bit!"

"Well," Maral said, stopping, "now that you ask, my back does feel a little sore."

Bilge nodded. "It's not too deep a cut. Still, that tree branch did a number on you. We should see to it that you suffer no further damage. We must seek out a special tree with a lineage that goes back two hundred million years. But to reach it, we will have to go out of our way."

Despite it being a bit of struggle, Maral sprang forward to once again reach her companion, who had kept walking as he talked. "Is it far?" she asked.

The gnome paused and looked toward the afternoon sun. "There's no way to tell exactly. The sun is on its way to setting. We must find the gingko tree, but it will take us in a roundabout way. In searching for the tree, we risk not getting back by nightfall. And under the cloud of darkness, it will be harder to detect hungry forest creatures on the prowl."

The fawn looked back toward her wound. Bilge, too, looked at her injury and shook his head. "But there's no choice, Maral. We must make the trek and take the risk. Your well-being should not be left to chance."

Dead twigs snapped under the gnome's feet as he hurried onward in a new direction—away from home. He pushed away thin branches with his arm, clearing a path big enough to let the fawn through so the foliage wouldn't brush against her open wound.

The sound of insects filled the dry air. Crickets and grasshoppers rubbed their spindly legs together and strummed noisy tunes.

The late-afternoon sun was warm but not bright under the canopy of forest trees. Bilge hummed as they walked, and Maral followed without a word, allowing the gnome to concentrate on looking for clues as to the whereabouts of the gingko tree.

Without ado, Bilge spoke, "The gingko tree will serve a two-fold purpose, my friend. Its fan like leaves will heal, and it will also impart a truth we might not have come across, had it not been for our needing its healing properties.

"Let me tell you a bit about the tree that we hope to find, Maral. Its history spans millions of years. Although the tree has endured for eons, the shape of its leaves and the color of its bark have hardly changed. What we will see today is what our ancestors saw millions of years ago. For this reason, some call the gingko a living fossil. Eh, despite living for ages, the tree has no relatives, and is a lonely one."

A gray squirrel ran past carrying something round and orange. Just then, an awful odor filled the air. The gnome turned up his nose to inhale the offensive scent.

"It's in the air, Maral. We are getting closer."

"What's in the air?" asked the fawn eagerly, as she stumbled over a rock.

"The wind carries the foul smell of the gingko fruit. We simply must continue in the direction from which the wind blows."

The gnome licked his index finger and then held it in midair to let the wind blow against it. "This way, Maral!"

Within a mere half hour, the pair walked upon dried-up leaves in the shape of small fans. Bilge kneeled to further inspect them. Picking one up, he laughed.

"Oh-oh! What have we here? It is none other than the fallen leaves of the gingko tree!" He peered at the clusters of trees around them. One with chipped, gray bark attracted his attention.

Maral scrunched up her nose and squeezed her eyes shut. "What *is* that horrible smell?"

The gnome walked straight to the tree with the gray bark. "We have found it, Maral. You smell the fruit of the gingko, and we will have your wound properly healed in no time."

Bilge set down his canteen and lantern, gathered some of the fruits strewn on the ground, and picked a few from its branches.

Then he searched the ground again. "A rock, Maral. I need a flat rock. Do you see any?"

Maral started looking too. "Nope."

The gnome twisted his head around. "Ah! This will do." He set down his stash of gingko fruits on a flat rock. Using another rock, he smashed them into a paste. Next, he untwisted the cap from his canteen and poured a bit of water into the paste.

"We have no oil to add to this paste, Maral, which is how the remedy is traditionally made, but the pond water will do. Now come on." He motioned for the fawn to come closer.

The gnome rubbed the paste into the fawn's wound. "This will take care of your injury. The paste has antibacterial properties. Your wound will get no worse, only better."

"It's soothing," said Maral. She bent her head down and started nibbling on the fallen fruits.

"They smell rotten, but these gingko fruits sure taste sweet!" said Maral between chomps.

"I know you're hungry, Maral," Bilge said, a warning in his tone, "but limit yourself to ten fruits to avoid the stomach pain and confusion that comes with ingesting more than that. Remember, eating too many gingko fruits won't be good for you, but just the right amount will heal you."

She continued munching but heeded the gnome's warning.

"I almost forgot!" said Bilge. "We have received the healing. Now it is time for the truth we have come to uncover."

The fawn lifted her head and turned her ears toward the gnome.

"What is it?"

"Be like the gingko tree: tolerant and healing. The tree is

immensely tolerant of all types of environmental conditions once it is firmly rooted. You, too, have clearly shown tolerance, enduring discomfort without complaint, and begun to heal in its aftermath. Admirably, your healing is taking place from both the outside *and* inside.

"Now, let us quickly be on our way, Maral, before the dangers of the dark begin to lurk about us."

Bilge picked up his lantern, strapped his canteen over his shoulder, and marched in the direction from whence they had come.

16
BE LIKE THE APPLE TREE

The gnome and fawn had traveled a good distance away from their planned route, and the part of the forest they now found themselves in was unfamiliar to the gnome. Though he'd lived under the forest trees all his life, he'd never had a reason to roam farther than necessary—until now.

Nurturing Maral was important to the gnome. The fawn was young and impressionable, and the gnome had always helped guide her, as any wise, older friend naturally would. Throughout their journey, though, he'd begun to see something in his young friend that would make her incredibly valuable to the well-being of the glorious forest world.

The animals of the forest had no one to encourage them to follow the life principles known to the gnome. Each creature fended for itself. The forest was a place of wildness. The virtues known to humanity were foreign to the inhabitants of the forest.

Only the wisest among the forest dwellers, like the gnome, knew of ideals such as peace, equality, and harmony. The gnome was old and had only a few more years to teach these ideals he prized so highly to some worthy creature. It was the fawn who had become his willing student.

The pair meandered toward a clearing that was open to the skies, unlike the rest of the forest through which they had trod. Here, trees blossomed, nourished by the ample sunlight.

Maral's stomach growled, and Bilge's ears perked up. "A fine feast you shall have soon, Maral. We are amid none other than the—"

Before Bilge could finish his sentence, Maral sprinted toward the orchard of apple trees and began to nosh on the hanging red fruit.

The gnome hobbled in her direction at his usual pace. "Ah, dwarf trees, just the right height from which to feed."

As Maral stuffed her empty belly, Bilge leaned against the trunk of a tree and drifted into a daydream. Several minutes later, Maral nudged her nose against the gnome's arm. He sputtered and blinked. "What, well, I say, you've had your fill?" he asked.

Maral's mouth was covered in bits of apple. She vigorously nodded.

"The apple tree is generous enough to offer its bountiful fruit. There are eight thousand varieties of apples. Can you imagine thousands of variations of palm-sized roundness? Yet each variety is blessed with integrity. Knowing its specialness, every apple is contented to be its true self, never mimicking another variety. I dare say, Maral, the apple tree has much more to offer us other than simply its fruit."

Maral blinked and looked at the gnome with wide eyes. Her cheeks were still stuffed with the apples.

"I suppose, Maral, you want to know what truths the apple tree holds?" he asked.

Maral nodded again. Bits of apple fell from the sides of her mouth.

"Be like the apple tree: generous and true. We see how its boughs give fruit, but its openhandedness comes from a place of wisdom. The entire forest realm relishes the apple's bounty: the joyous songbirds, the sleepy bears awakening from hibernation, the scampering mice led by voracious appetites, and the masked raccoons. How empty we'd be without the true generosity of the apple tree. It understands its value and gives of itself."

Maral twisted her nose, a question in her expression. "But why do we have to be wise to be generous?" she managed to say after swallowing a bite.

The gnome turned from the fruit hanging on the tree to spy the fawn. "If I were to be generous and give you a pair of my finest clogs, what would you do with them?"

Maral dipped her head and then looked up awkwardly at the gnome. "I . . . I don't know. I'd wear them?"

"You would try! My dear, you'd wear them for about five seconds, and then as soon as you took one hop, they'd fall right off your hooves. My clogs are not made for a fawn's hooves, Maral. Though generosity would be my intention, it would be inconvenient for you to receive such a gift. Even my most comfortable clogs would do you absolutely no good. So, you see, a gift must be given with wisdom. Only then can it be meaningfully embraced by the heart of the recipient."

"Is that why you give us alfalfa sprouts every morning? To be generous?"

"Quite right you are, Maral. It's a simple gift, but it comes from a place of benevolence and wisdom. What would you do if each morning I placed shiny gold nuggets, brilliant green emeralds, and shimmering rubies in the basket for all the forest deer?"

"Gold nuggets, emeralds, and rubies would be rather hard to digest. I prefer alfalfa sprouts—they're softer and far more delicious."

Bilge laughed heartily and patted Maral on her furry head. "Let it also be known, Maral, that generosity is never a onetime gesture. True generosity is giving over a lifetime."

The companions leisurely circled the orchard. "You feed us forest creatures over our lifetimes," said the fawn with a spring in her step. "I remember the taste of the first alfalfa sprouts I had from your basket. They were delightful and have been ever since."

"Indeed. I am glad to hear it. Now you know the meaning of real generosity."

The gnome glanced up at the low-hanging fruits. "Now, more lessons are to be had from the splendid apple tree."

"Oh? Like what?"

"Well, looking at this stunning piece of fruit, I can say with certainty that the apple is happy to be itself. Too often creatures strive to outdo others purely for the sake of outdoing them. Whatever for? We are surrounded by beings who trample on one another to get ahead. It is the opposite of progress to crush another."

The gnome reached up to the dwarf apple tree and plucked a fruit. "But not the apple tree, Maral. The apple tree dwells in its own splendid nature, and gives what it has—apples, in its case. The ability to recognize unique personal strengths and utilize them to the fullest is to be prized in our world."

He rotated the apple in his hand and admired its brilliant sheen. "Being true to oneself is unlike any other joy."

Maral gulped the last few bits of apple in her mouth and let out a loud burp. She giggled.

The gnome chuckled and looked around. Luscious apples were scattered over the ground, and plenty more heavy, ripened fruit hung low on the trees' branches.

"We mustn't let all this bounty go to waste!"

Maral cleared her throat. "Can we take some apples home?"

"Of course! We shall make pies, tarts, muffins . . ." His voice trailed off as he stooped to pick up the apples that had fallen from the tree. Maral also bit off a few apples from the branches.

Once the gnome's pockets were bursting with apples, the friends resumed their journey home.

"You know, Maral, I've got this tantalizing recipe for apple frangipane tarts," said Bilge with a smile. "It has a shortbread crust and pieces of apple baked right into its center. Slivers of almonds are sprinkled over the top. Heavenly, just heavenly."

"Mmm, sounds delicious!"

"It won't be much longer until we can bake it! The freshest apples make the tastiest tarts." The gnome wobbled as he walked, his pockets stuffed with big apples.

17
BE LIKE THE CANOPY OF THE BANYAN TREE

It wasn't long before they reached another clearing. Maral and the gnome stopped in their tracks. What stood before them was another masterpiece of nature, and like others in the forest they had seen, a gigantic one.

Maral spoke in a hushed tone, overcome. "It's amazing. A thousand tree trunks. But look!" She pointed. "No other plants grow in this grove."

"Ah, correction, Maral. This is not a grove of a thousand slender trees. It is one spectacular tree called the banyan tree. Its thousand branches grow downward, like roots, which appear like a grove of trees. And it is the way of the banyan tree to seize the ground around it and remain victorious over all surrounding life. It will not let anything else grow under it."

"That seems sort of selfish," said the fawn with a frown.

"The banyan tree is a tree all for itself, a tree among trees. A forest unto itself," said Bilge. "It is the sole ruler over the ground upon which it grows. Yet it is a wish-fulfilling tree. It will grant you what you most desire."

Maral scraped her hoof against the dirt and looked downward. "My wish, I believe, has already been granted."

"Oh?" said the gnome with a twist of his head. "Why, Maral, that is splendid! I hope our journey today has had something to do with your fulfillment."

The fawn smiled shyly.

"Still, Maral, we have not yet reached home, and the forest has many more truths to share. See, we can even learn from the banyan tree. The spectacular sight before us inspires us to be like the canopy of the banyan tree: stretching to the heavens."

Bilge craned his neck. "There's much the heavens can reveal to us before we reach it!"

Maral's eyes grew wide. "Can there be a heaven on earth?"

"Oh, Maral, you ask a meaningful question," said the gnome. "Now, let's see. I must dust off the boxes of knowledge stored in the deepest parts of my mind."

The gnome looked down to his feet, rubbed his beard, then glanced up to the sky again. "Ah, yes, I remember.

It is said that the banyan tree's branches are gifts from the heavens. Its thousands of branches reach downward to give blessings to all life on earth. So, you could say, parts of the earth are an extension of the heavens. Anyhow, we make the small plot of earth we are given either a heaven or a hell. It is up to each one of us to choose how well we till our soil."

"We are lucky to be in the midst of the banyan tree," said Maral, in awe.

"And fortunate to receive its continuous blessings," said the gnome. "As we stand before the otherworldly banyan tree, let it be known that it can deliver to us only otherworldly gifts. By the example of its high-reaching canopy, the tree encourages us to move beyond earthly pleasures and aspire for spiritual notions. In doing so, we may be fit to enter the realm of the most blessed of all."

Maral looked at her friend. "Has it always offered this message?"

Bilge nodded. "There is no doubt, Maral. The banyan tree has been the center of attention for hundreds of years in various parts of our forest world. Important discussions, like the one we're having now, have taken place under it. Weary travelers, such as migrating animals, have taken refuge from the sun beneath it. Its message is well received by anyone who is open and willing to accept it."

The gnome looked long toward the reddish ball of fire lingering on the horizon. "Better come along now. We should be home by dark."

18
BE LIKE THE BOULDER

*D*usk settled in quickly, making the gnome's lantern more valuable than ever. Thankfully, his tiny hut soon came into view. But before the pair reached the safety of home, Bilge stopped before a gigantic boulder.

"At the start of our journey, I'd have thought that a boulder couldn't offer us truths," said Maral. "But now I'm sure it must. This journey has led to a whole lot of discovery!"

With a chuckle, Bilge illuminated the massive gray stone. It stood ten feet high and was half the width of its height. The lantern's light revealed only a small portion of the boulder's surface.

"Quite right, Maral. This boulder has been sitting here patiently for eons. The likes of these majestic natural wonders have been brought to the forest by glacial ice."

Maral's eyes sparkled in the near darkness, like fireflies in July. "Our forest was filled with ice?"

"Oh yes, Maral, a long time ago. In fact, there was a time when most of the planet was covered in ice. When the earth warmed, the ice disappeared, except for at the poles. What we see here was deposited by the glacial forces millions of years ago."

"It's a wonder that it's still here," said the fawn, "perhaps remaining just as it looked many years ago."

"Indeed, the boulder is as it always was, although slightly worn by erosion. Nevertheless, it has happily remained here for millennia. You, Maral, have the gifts of the boulder."

"Oh no, no! I hardly stay in one place. I hop around—"

"Of course," Bilge interrupted, "but you see, Maral, you have discovered what it is to be like the boulder: steadfast and loyal. You've stood, or perhaps hopped, by my side the entire journey. You are genuinely faithful, and you are resolute in your desire to learn nature's truths—truths that will give you your heart's deepest wish."

Maral started to smile, then her eyelids drooped and she yawned a big yawn.

The gnome and the fawn made it back to the hut just as the crescent moon rose and the nighttime stars began dancing and glimmering in the darkened sky.

"Ah! Back at last," said Bilge. "And we made it in one piece. Or I suppose I should say two pieces—you and I." He set down his lantern on the table inside his hut. Maral stumbled inside, half-asleep, and settled on the gnome's rug in front of the fireplace. After lighting the fire, Bilge plopped onto his bed.

"Goodnight, Maral. We have one more truth to uncover when you awake."

But Maral was already snoozing.

19
BE LIKE THE DANDELION

The next day, the sun rose in a clear sky. The playful rays of light coming through the hut's window tickled Maral's eyelids, waking her.

"Good morning, Maral!" said Bilge. He was busily preparing a breakfast of griddle cakes and dandelions.

"Good day to you," said Maral, her voice gravelly with sleep.

"Have yourself some breakfast and then meet me outside. We shall see what's in the garden."

The fawn gobbled up the hot breakfast, as if she hadn't eaten a solid meal in an entire day. Then with crumbs on her nose, Maral strode outside.

The gnome had set out a basket of clover, alfalfa, and dandelion, as he usually did. The forest deer pranced nearby and trotted over to accept the breakfast, as they usually did.

Bilge gently patted the visiting deer on their backs, some of whom, since they had morning breakfasts together, were friendly with Maral. Then the gnome turned his attention to Maral.

"And now, Maral, one last truth that the forest has been waiting to reveal—a truth you have faced every morning without realizing it." Bilge picked a dandelion from his basket.

"Here is the dandelion." The gnome twirled the yellow-petaled flower between his fingers. "This is a flower that brings hope and happiness. This little dandelion will make your wishes for prosperity come true. This is a flower of new beginnings."

Maral stretched her neck out, as if about to chomp on the delicate petals.

The gnome laughed and pulled his hand back. "You can munch on the dandelion, Maral. But first, know what it is to be like the dandelion: hopeful and happy. I dare say, my friend, you have become the cheery sort!"

"Oh, I have!" replied the fawn. Her eyes glistened brightly—no longer with tears, but with happiness—and she smiled radiantly. She had a higher bounce in her trot.

"And who do you want to be now?" asked the gnome. His arm inched closer to Maral's neck, and she quickly reached out and nibbled the dandelion.

"Oh, myself!"

The gnome smiled gently. The creases around his eyes deepened. "Very good, Maral. You've been on a long journey through the depths of our great forest and learned a great deal. One day is a long time in the life of a young fawn."

"Sure is!" said Maral. She happily chewed on the last petals of the flower.

"The gifts of humankind are available to all life on earth. And these truths that show us the way to happiness are found in natural places, where life is blessed with the majestic freedom to live to its full glory."

The fawn nodded eagerly. Then one of the visiting deer nuzzled her nose, and Maral sped off with her. Both the fawn and deer laughed and smiled and played in the fields, as the gnome held his belly and laughed joyfully.

20
AFTER THE QUEST

*I*n the months after her journey, Maral was reminded of the natural truths within the forest that Bilge had brought to light. Although her first trip with the gnome was complete, the fawn's inner voyage continued. She foraged under the redwood, humbled yet inspired by its strength. She held her head high as the wind blew, feeling how adaptable and resolute it is. She placed one hoof on the boulder, touched by its commitment and constancy.

More and more, Maral blossomed into the wisest and most fulfilled of forest animals. She often gave advice to her forest mates—the deer, the rabbits, and even the timid skunks—all of whom listened with great intent and admiration. She was a prized friend of the forest dwellers.

Then one fine day, eight months after their journey, Bilge gathered all the nearby animals. He stood on a fallen tree trunk to make an announcement.

"A lesson has truly been learned when the student becomes the teacher. Maral," he said, gesturing to his friend in the crowd, "please step up."

Maral slowly approached the tree trunk. At one year old, the white spots on her back had disappeared, and her body was bigger and muscular. The wound she had sustained many months earlier had completely healed; the scar on her skin was buried underneath a healthy coat of silky brown fur.

The gnome held a colorful, fragrant garland of flowers, and as he spoke again, he placed it on Maral's head.

"I and the forest animals wish you the happiest first birthday, Maral. Over the months, you have shown yourself to be capable and compassionate, one who is able to win the affections of many. I have seen how you are self-respecting and dignified, humble and forgiving, and hardy and brave. You have found fulfillment—one of life's most priceless experiences—and I wish for you to show others how to find it within themselves."

The forest animals whistled and cheered loudly.

Maral acknowledged Bilge's hope with a nod, and, as she did so, the garland of flowers slipped a few inches down her forehead. The fawn wiggled her head so that the flowers no longer covered her eyes. Witnessing the spectacle, the gnome couldn't help but laugh.

Stepping on the trunk, Maral cleared her throat. "Since you've all gathered here, I have something to say to each of you. The morning I started my journey to the ends of the forest and back, I wished for lasting happiness. At the same time, I was gripped with fear, equally afraid of the unknown and the known. I was terrified of the blinding light, the mysterious darkness, the shrill noise, the deafening silence. Now I know that fear and happiness cannot live together.

"But I wished to feel joy more than I cared to live with fear. Bilge and the forest guided me each step of the way. Though we followed no trail, everywhere I turned, there was a hidden path that clearly led me. A path is there for everyone who pays attention. By the end of it all—and there really is no end to the truths our forest carries—I felt my heart beat carefree. Instead of fear, I felt courage. Fresh confidence replaced my suffocating doubts. The birth of courage and newfound strength were the foundations for my fulfillment.

"Yes, unwittingly, I faced the wicked Kotu, but in the midst of this danger, I discovered an unexpected will to live—a blessing in disguise. Instinctually, I relied on this universal life force the rest of the way. Now, here I am to tell you that happiness comes and goes, but fulfillment— which is not for the faint of heart—is a deep and lasting joy. If a fawn like me can wake up the courage within, even the wee forest creatures can too."

After Maral spoke, a long silence filled the forest. The timid skunk started to clap with some hesitation, then others joined. In seconds, the entire group of animals stood up and gave the fawn several rounds of thunderous applause. Maral looked at Bilge and smiled, knowing that the animals had understood.

Over the next two years, Bilge continued to set out a basket of clover, alfalfa, and dandelion, as he usually did. The forest deer, including Maral, came to nibble on the greens, as they usually did.

Then one morning, the gnome did not set out his basket of greens. Maral and the forest deer stood next to Bilge's hut for a while. When he did not come out, the deer hopped away, looking for food elsewhere in the forest—but not Maral, who stayed.

Maral nestled in the grass, waiting for her friend. A half hour passed, and he still did not appear. Maral gingerly stood up on her four legs, walked up to his front door, and nudged it open with her nose.

Bilge lay in his bed, his arms at his sides and his soft blue blanket covering his body. "Maral, it is so nice to see you, my friend," he said with a crackle in his voice. He managed a weak smile.

Maral slowly stepped closer to the gnome's bed and stood by his side. Bilge turned his face slightly to look at the fawn.

"A beautiful life ends with a beautiful death."

"Please don't go," said Maral as tears flooded her doe eyes.

"You cannot ask me to stay, Maral. It is like asking the sun to rise from the west." Bilge, still speaking faintly, continued, "You will be just fine, Maral. We shall meet again in the eternal forest. Maral . . ."

Bilge's eyes closed. Maral nuzzled against the gnome's arm, but he remained still. The fawn noticed a peaceful smile had spread across the gnome's face. At that moment, the downy white clouds parted in the blue sky. A golden gleam of the morning sun burst through the parting and into the hut. Maral looked through the window and into the sky, stretching her neck like the canopy of the banyan tree. It was as if the heavens had opened to embrace the spirit of the gnome.

"Yes," whispered Maral, "we shall meet again in the eternal forest." She dropped to her knees and sobbed.

But the gnome was not entirely gone. Just like the fallen redwood tree that nourishes the soil after it returns to the ground, Bilge's profound lessons continued to nurture Maral. Her surroundings were evocative reminders of the natural truths that Bilge had taken great time and care to show her. Deeply saddened by the loss of her trusted confidant, Maral reflected on his earlier lesson of the crushed, humble violet: a passing is all in the natural circle of life.

Days went by, and Maral gradually regained her strength and joy—a joy she knew the gnome would want her to protect and grow within herself. Each night since then, Maral lit the gnome's lantern and hung it outside his porch to serve as a gentle reminder to all the forest creatures that nature's truths endure, continually offering the light of hope.

Maral remained a compassionate friend, a gentle guide, and a strong supporter to the forest creatures. Her dedication to the life within the forest ensured that the unwitting animals, the tender plants, and the hardy trees flourished. Benevolence pervaded the forest, more so than the brilliant rays of sunlight through the canopies of towering trees, and all was well within the forest realm.

Thank you for reading
Maral and the Wisdom of the Forest: A Quest for Truth.

If you enjoyed this inspirational novella, please consider leaving a review and help other readers discover enriching tales.

Visit my author website:
www.riyapresents.com